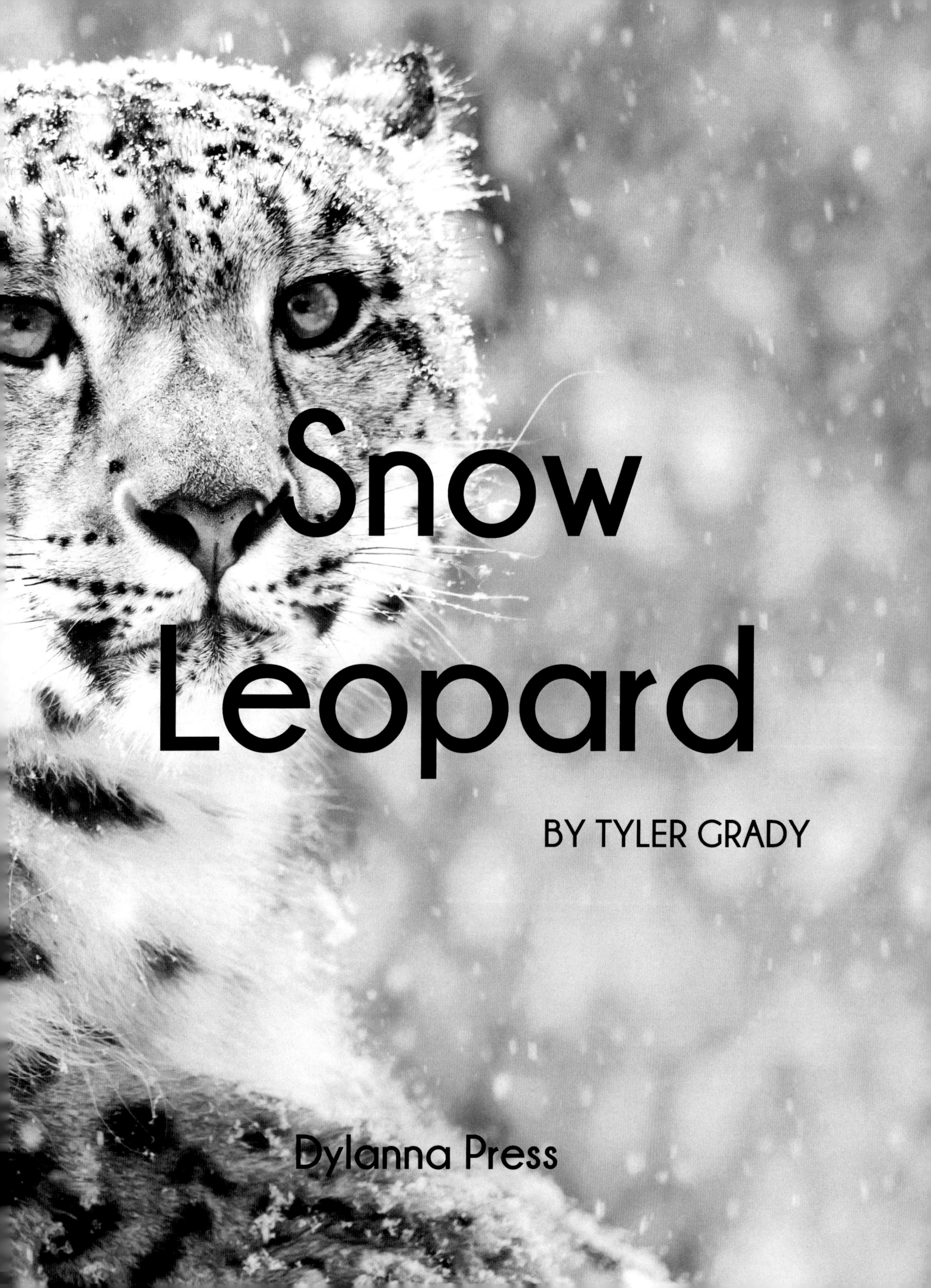

Snow Leopard

BY TYLER GRADY

Dylanna Press

Snow Leopards are **mammals** that can be found in the mountains of northern and central Asia including the countries of China, Nepal, Bhutan, India, Kazakhstan, Kyrgyzstan, Pakistan, Russia, Afghanistan, Tajikistan, Uzbekistan, and Mongolia.

They are related to lions, tigers, and other types of cats. Their scientific name is *Panthera uncia* (or *Uncia uncia*) and they belong to the Felidae family.

---

mammals – warm-blooded animals with hair or fur that give birth to live young

One of the most **elusive** members of the big cat family, the snow leopard is rarely seen in the wild and is known as the "ghost of the mountain."

They weigh from 60 to 120 pounds (27 to 54 kg) and average 3 to 4 feet (1 to 1.2 m) in length with an additional 2 to 3 foot (.6 to .9 meter) tail. Males are slightly larger than females.

Snow leopards have powerful, compact bodies with shorter legs, large heads, small rounded ears, and a long, bushy tail. They have thick, light gray fur tinged with yellow, and are covered with black **rosettes.**

---

elusive – difficult to find

rosettes – irregular-shaped spots

The snow leopard's **habitat** is the mountains of Central Asia. This includes the Himalayan Mountains, where they are found above the tree line at **elevations** of 3,000 to 5,400 meters (10,000 to 18,000 feet) above sea level.

In these areas the climate is cold and dry without much vegetation. They prefer areas with steep rocky cliffs and **ravines** from which they can get a clear view of their prey and surrounding areas. Their thick fur allows them to live in such harsh conditions and also helps them blend into the landscape.

---

habitat – surroundings or conditions in which an animal lives

elevation – distance above sea level

ravine – a deep narrow steep-sided valley

The snow leopard has many physical **adaptations** to its environment.

- Large chest and lungs help them breathe in the thin air of the mountains
- Deep nasal cavity warms cold air before it enters lungs
- Extra-large front paws act like snowshoes, keeping them from sinking into deep snow
- Shorter front and strong, muscular back legs allow them to leap up to 45 feet (14 meters)
- Long, thick tail helps them keep their balance and also wraps around body for warmth
- Thick fur provides warmth and camouflage
- Excellent eyesight allows them to spot prey
- Small ears help to prevent heat loss

---

adaptations – ways in which a species becomes fitted into its natural environment to increase its chance of survival

Snow leopards are **carnivores**. Their favorite food sources are wild sheep and ibex (a wild goat), but they also will eat smaller animals such as marmots, pika, rabbits, and even birds. Occasionaly they will eat wild grass and other vegetation.

Snow leopards will eat a medium-size animal such as a sheep over the course of several days. They will stay nearby and protect their kill from **scavengers**, eating every few hours until it is gone. They will wait several days before hunting again.

---

carnivore – animal that only eats meat

scavenger – animal that feeds on what another animal has left

Snow leopards are **solitary** hunters who typically hunt at dawn and dusk.

They prefer to stalk and **ambush** their prey by waiting in hiding and slowly creeping up on their target. When the animal is within striking distance, typically 20 to 50 feet (6-15 m) away, they will make a brief charge and pounce. Once the animal is down, the leopard will bite its throat or back of the neck.

Snow leopards are **opportunistic** hunters and will prey on domestic livestock. This creates conflict with local human populations.

---

solitary – done or existing alone

ambush – surprise attack from a concealed position

opportunistic – to take advantage of circumstances

Snow leopards are **monogamous**, having only one mate per season. The mating season takes place between January and the middle of March. Snow leopards reach maturity between three and four years old.

Male and female snow leopards only stay together for a few days. The male leopard then leaves and does not take part in raising the cubs.

Pregnancy lasts between 95 and 105 days, with birth taking place from April to June. Female snow leopards typically have two to three cubs at a time.

---

monogamous – staying with one mate at a time

A mother snow leopard will seek out a protected den to give birth to her cubs in. Cubs are small and helpless when they are born and don't even open their eyes for the first week. The cubs will remain in the den for the first couple of months.

The mother leopard takes care of them by herself, keeping them safe and providing food. Snow leopard mothers are very protective and will stay with their cubs almost all of the time, leaving only to hunt.

At about three months the cubs will start following along with their mother and begin to learn to hunt. Cubs stay with their mother for about two years before they are ready to go out into the world alone.

Snow leopards love to sleep!

They average about 18 hours per day. This is needed to preserve and recharge their energy levels.

They are **crepuscular** animals who sleep most the day and are most active at dawn and dusk, as well as in the night.

Their preferred sleeping spots are in high, protected areas with good views of the surrounding landscape. In order to keep warm while asleep they will wrap their large, furry tail around their body.

---

crepuscular – most active and dawn and dusk

Snow Leopards are **solitary** animals who spend the majority of their lives alone, with the exception of a mother leopard and her cubs. Adult snow leopards only interact during mating. Young, newly independent leopards may stay together briefly with littermates while establishing territories.

Snow leopards are territorial and will roam across and defend a range large enough to provide them with an adequate supply of food. A male leopard's range can overlap with several female snow leopards. To mark their **territory**, leopards will leave scent marks and scratches on rocks and trees.

Unlike other big cats, snow leopards do not roar. Instead, they communicate using **vocalizations** such as yowls, chuffs, growls, and even purrs.

---

solitary – done or existing alone

territory – area of land that belongs to an animal

vocalizations – the sounds an animal makes

The average lifespan of a snow leopard in the wild is 10 to 12 years. They can live twenty years or more in captivity.

It is hard to know exactly how many snow leopards are left in the wild but scientists estimate there are between 4,000 and 6,500 remaining as of 2022.

Due to stricter anti-poaching laws the snow leopard population has increased in recent years and they are no longer listed as an endangered species. They are now a considered a **vulnerable species**. While improved they are still not out of danger.

---

vulnerable species – species considered to be facing a high risk of extinction in the wild

Snow leopards are at the top of the food chain. A fully grown snow leopard faces no predators in its natural habitat, making them **apex predators**. However, wolves have been known to prey on cubs.

Humans are by far the biggest threat to snow leopards. Expanding human populations lead to habitat loss and fragmentation. Snow leopards who kill livestock are often killed by farmers in retaliation.

Poaching also contributes to snow leopard deaths. They are hunted for their beautiful fur and as trophies.

Another risk facing snow leopards is **climate change**. As the planet continues to get warmer, their habitat will continue to shrink.

---

apex predator – an animal at the top of the food chain

poaching – illegal killing and trafficking of animals

climate change – long-term changes in weather patterns

Snow Leopards are beautiful and elusive animals. They are sacred animals to the people of the Himalayas and symbolize strength and agility.

Unfortunately, snow leopards continued existence remains in doubt due to loss of habitat, hunting, and the ongoing threat of climate change.

Conservation efforts are underway but it remains to be seen if this amazing big cat can survive in the coming decades.

---

conservation – protecting natural resources for future generations

Word Search

J O S R R A V I N E S I A A H R
R H E S E T T E S O R Y M S G I
A A I A J J L B S J M T E V W O
L Q C M F D F D E V Y Y S B A D
U J E C G F D H P R Y N M H I Z
C E P O A C A W A H O X T I B E
S L S V P I C T V I H A H M U X
U U P M E P I A T K T H S A Z T
P S P A A L O A R I S V U L S I
E I D W O M T R B N B S B A U N
R V J S L P M A T O I I M Y K C
C E H T A L H A H U S V A A K T
T G J D Q L B J L G N H O S W I
W U A A U M L W X S F I K R E O
L V X N E A D I L E F Z S F E N
S T E R R I T O R Y L L K T W S
V B S C A V E N G E R S R L I Q
E F K N O I T A V R E S N O C C

ADAPTATIONS
AMBUSH
CARNIVORES
CONSERVATION
CREPUSCULAR
ELUSIVE
EXTINCTION
FELIDAE
HABITAT
HIMALAYAS
MAMMALS
OPPORTUNISTIC
RAVINES
ROSETTES
SCAVENGERS
SOLITARY
SPECIES
TERRITORY

INDEX

Published by Dylanna Press an imprint of Dylanna Publishing, Inc.

Author: Tyler Grady

Printed in the U.S.A.

Made in the USA
Monee, IL
18 November 2024